THE LIBRARY OF
WOLVES AND WILD DOGS ™

THE RED WOLF

Fred H. Harrington

The Rosen Publishing Group's
PowerKids Press ™
New York

To Howard McCarley and Glynn Riley, two red wolf biologists from 'down south' who journeyed up north to Ely, Minnesota, back in the early 1970s to talk about red wolves and listen to gray wolves howl. All the red wolves alive today owe a debt to their early efforts.

Published in 2002 by The Rosen Publishing Group, Inc.
29 East 21st Street, New York, NY 10010

First Edition

Book Design: Michael de Guzman
Project Editor: Emily Raabe

Photo Credits: p. 4 (wolves) © Lee Kuhn/FPG International; p. 4 (map) © MapArt (digital manipulation by Michael de Guzman); p. 7 © Lynda Richardson/CORBIS; p. 8 © Nancy Rotenberg/Earth Scenes; p. 11 (wolf) © James H. Robinson/Animals Animals; p.11 (coyote) © Glen Rowell/CORBIS; p. 12 © C. C. Lockwood/Animals Animals; pp. 14, 20 © U. S. Fish and Wildlife Service; p. 15 (raccoon) © Joe McDonald/CORBIS; p. 15 (deer) © D. Robert Franz/CORBIS; p. 16 © Stouffer Prod./Animals Animals; p. 19 (wolf) © Stouffer Prod./Animals Animals; p. 19 (coyote) © W. Perry Conway/CORBIS; p. 19 (map) © MapArt (digital manipulation by Michael de Guzman); p. 22 © Lynda Richardson/CORBIS.

Harrington, Fred H.
     The red wolf / by Fred H. Harrington.
          p. cm. — (The library of wolves and wild dogs)
     ISBN 0-8239-5765-9
     1. Red wolf—Juvenile literature. [1. Red wolf. 2. Wolves.] I. Title.
     II. Series.
QL737.C22 H368 2002
599.733—dc21
                                                                    00-011793

Manufactured in the United States of America

Contents

North Carolina

Wild Dogs and Wolves

There are many kinds of wild dogs living all around the world. Dingoes, for example, live in Australia. African hunting dogs roam southern Africa. Bush dogs are found in South America. Asiatic wild dogs live in southeast Asia. Most of these wild dogs are very different from the domestic dogs that live with us. The wild dogs that are most like our domestic dogs are the wolves. There are three wolf **species**. These are the gray wolves, the red wolves, and the Ethiopian wolves. Gray wolves are the most common of the three wolf species. They are found all around the northern hemisphere. Both Ethiopian wolves and red wolves are very rare. Ethiopian wolves live only in the country of Ethiopia, in Africa. Red wolves remain only in the state of North Carolina.

 Red wolves today live only in a small region of North Carolina, not far from the Atlantic Ocean.

Red Wolves and Gray Wolves

Red wolves are like gray wolves in many ways. Red wolves live in packs and hunt **prey** animals such as white-tailed deer, just like gray wolves do. They also care for their puppies and howl to protect their territory, like gray wolves do. In other ways, red wolves are different from gray wolves. They have more reddish fur than gray wolves do. They are also much smaller than gray wolves. Adults weigh only 40 to 90 pounds (18 to 41 kg). Adult gray wolves weigh between 80 and 120 pounds (36 to 54 kg). Differences such as weight and fur color show that red wolves are not just another kind of gray wolf. Some scientists believe that red wolves are a separate species of wolf, like the Ethiopian wolf that lives in Africa.

This is a pair of red wolves. Red wolves live in family groups called packs. Each pack is made up of a mother, a father, and their children.

Red Wolves Lose Their Land

Red wolves once lived throughout southeastern North America. They could be found from Pennsylvania to Florida, and west to Texas and Oklahoma. Red wolves were probably the first wolves in North America to meet European settlers. As people settled in places such as Virginia, the Carolinas, and Florida, they cut the forests to make their farms and **plantations**. People also killed many of the prey animals, such as white-tailed deer, that the red wolves needed. With less **habitat** to live in and fewer prey to hunt, red wolves became very rare. People also killed many red wolves. They believed the wolves were a threat to domestic animals and wildlife. By 1970, red wolves were left in only a small area of Louisiana and eastern Texas.

In this photograph, it is easy to see where the forest has been cut down to make room for pastureland.

Red Wolves Meet Coyotes

Red wolves faced another threat, as well. That threat was **hybridization**. A **hybrid** is a mix of two species. For example, when a horse and a donkey mate, their baby is a mule. A mule is different from both of its parents. Coyotes and red wolves are different species, but they are closely related. Red wolves began to **mate** with coyotes on the western edge of their range. When they mated, they had

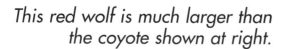

This red wolf is much larger than the coyote shown at right.

puppies that were bigger than coyotes, but smaller than red wolves. When the hybrid puppies grew up, they mated with coyotes because many coyotes lived in the same habitat. Their puppies looked even more like coyotes. By the mid-1970s, only a few dozen true red wolves were left in the wild. Red wolves quickly were becoming **extinct**.

The coyote (right) has a grayer coat of fur than the red wolf (left).

Saving Red Wolves

In 1973, scientists decided to catch all the red wolves that still lived in the wild so they would not mate with coyotes. The scientists found only 14 red wolves living in the wild. Red wolves were terribly close to extinction! The scientists brought the red wolves into **captivity**. In captivity, the red wolves mated and had puppies. In fewer than 10 years, more than 60 red wolves were living in captivity. In 1977, a scientist named Howard McCarley went back to eastern Texas, one of the last places where red wolves had lived in the wild. Dr. McCarley found only coyotes and hybrids living there. True red wolves had completely disappeared from the wild. By breeding red wolves in captivity, scientists saved them from extinction, and just in time!

 This red wolf is part of the Red Wolf Recovery Project on Horn Island, off the coast of Mississippi.

A New Home for Red Wolves

Scientists knew that red wolves needed a new home in the wild. Finding a new home took planning. Red wolves hunt small **mammals** such as raccoons and rabbits and bigger mammals such as white-tailed deer. Their new home had to have a lot of prey for food. It also had to be far away from people and farm animals, because red wolves sometimes kill animals such as sheep and chickens. The scientists did not want farmers getting mad at the wolves. Finally, the new home had to be far away

This is the Alligator River National Wildlife Refuge in North Carolina, where red wolves found their home.

from coyotes, so the wolves and coyotes would not mate. Alligator River National Wildlife Refuge in eastern North Carolina was chosen as the red wolves' new home. It had plenty of food but was far away from farms and coyotes. Thirty-six red wolves were released in Alligator River National Wildlife Refuge from 1987 to 1992.

The raccoon is a popular prey animal for the red wolf.

The white-tailed deer makes up 50 percent of the red wolf's diet.

Learning to Be Wild

Red wolves had a lot to learn when they were released into the wild. When they lived in captivity, people fed them. In the wild they had to feed themselves, but they were not very good hunters. They also had to learn to avoid people and cars. Many red wolves had trouble **adapting** to life in the wild. Some of them had to be recaptured and brought back into captivity. Others were killed by cars or drowned in rivers. Some red wolves **survived**, though. The red wolves that did survive mated and had puppies. These puppies were the first red wolves born in the wild in more than 10 years! The puppies quickly learned how to survive. They became good hunters and avoided people and roads. Today almost all of the red wolves living in the wild were born there.

 These red wolf pups were born in the wild.

Keeping Red Wolves Safe

About 100 red wolves were living in the wild in North Carolina in 2000. Does that mean that red wolves are saved from extinction? Unfortunately, no. Red wolves still face the threat of hybridization with coyotes. When scientists first moved red wolves to North Carolina in 1987, coyotes did not live there. That made North Carolina a good place for red wolves to live. Today coyotes live in many parts of North Carolina. Some coyotes even live close to where red wolves live. In fact, some coyotes have mated already with red wolves. There aren't many hybrid puppies yet, but scientists worry that many more coyotes will start to mate with red wolves, just like they did when red wolves lived in Texas. Scientists are planning new ways to keep coyotes and red wolves apart, so they won't mate and have hybrid puppies.

The red wolf (left) and the coyote (right) now must share the state of North Carolina.

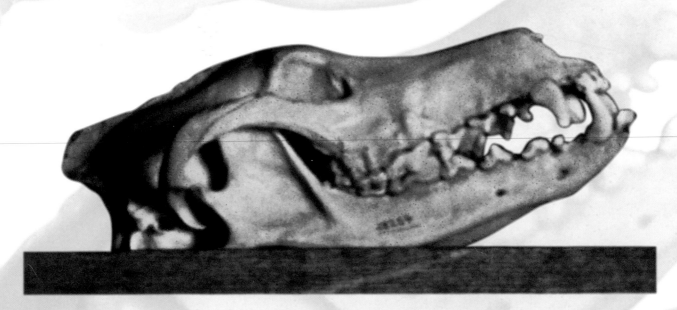

Bones and Genes

Coyotes are not the only problem facing red wolves today. Some scientists don't believe that red wolves ever existed at all as a separate species! Why? The answer depends on how scientists tell one species of animal from another. Some scientists study animals' **genes** to tell species apart. Genes are the parts of an animal's cells that tell the animal's body how to grow. Red wolf genes are similar to both gray wolf genes and coyote genes, so scientists studying genes believe that red wolves are just hybrids between gray wolves and coyotes. Other scientists look at the bones of animals, especially their **skulls**. Red wolf skulls and gray wolf skulls are different, so some scientists believed that red wolves and gray wolves are indeed different species. Is the red wolf a separate species, or a hybrid? Scientists don't know yet.

The gray wolf skull shown here (top) *is much larger than the red wolf skull* (bottom).

What Red Wolves Have Taught People

The red wolf's future is uncertain. Scientists will have to work hard to keep coyotes from mating with the red wolves now living in the wild. Scientists also have to figure out just how red wolves are related to coyotes and gray wolves. The release of red wolves in North Carolina, however, has taught scientists important lessons about how to return wolves to the wild. These lessons have helped scientists to return gray wolves to Yellowstone National Park in Wyoming, and to the southwest in Arizona and New Mexico. Someday they may help scientists bring gray wolves back to wild areas in the northeastern United States, such as the Adirondack Mountains in New York. Whatever becomes of the red wolf, it has helped other wolves return to the wild.

Glossary

adapting (uh-DAP-ting) Changing to fit new conditions.

captivity (kap-TIH-vih-tee) When an animal lives in a zoo or an aquarium instead of in the wild.

extinct (ik-STINKT) No longer existing.

genes (JEENZ) Many tiny parts in the center of a cell. Genes tell your cells how your body will look and act.

habitat (HA-bih-tat) The surroundings where an animal or plant naturally lives.

hybrid (HY-brid) An animal that is a mixture of two different species.

hybridization (hy-brih-dih-ZAY-shun) When a male and a female of two different species mate and have babies.

mammals (MAH-mulz) Warm-blooded animals that have a backbone, are often covered with hair, breathe air, and feed milk to their young.

mate (MAYT) When a male and a female join together to make babies.

plantations (plan-TAY-shunz) Very large farms where crops such as tobacco and cotton are grown. Many plantation owners used slaves to work these farms.

prey (PRAY) An animal that is hunted by another animal for food.

skulls (SKULZ) The bones in an animal's or a person's head that protect its brain.

species (SPEE-sheez) A single kind of plant or animal. For example, all people are one species.

survived (sur-VYVD) Lived longer than; stayed alive.

Index

Web Sites

To learn more about red wolves, check out these Web sites:

http://endangered.fws.gov/kids/index.html

http://southeast.fws.gov/pubs/alwolf.pdf

www.outer-banks.com/alligator-river/redwolf.html